Make the Most of You

LIME TREE BOOKS

Make the Most of You

170 ways to be the best you can

Patrick Lindsay

LIME TREE BOOKS

SYDNEY

For
Lisa, Nathan, Kate, Sarah, Nic & Josh

LIME TREE BOOKS

Published in 2013 by Lime Tree Books

LIME TREE BOOKS

Lime Tree Books
Suite 1401
93 Pacific Highway
North Sydney NSW 2060
Australia
www.patricklindsay.com.au

A Cataloguing-in-Publication entry is available from the catalogue of the National Library of Australia at www.nla.gov.au
Make The Most of You: 170 ways to be the best you can
ISBN 9780987582607

Jacket design and illustration by Nicole Watts, Red Cloud Digital
Typeset in 10/12pt The Sans Ultra Light by Red Cloud Digital
Editor Felicity Lewis, Wordigirl
Printed and bound in China by C&C Offset Printing Co Ltd

Look for depth

Our world pushes us towards shallowness.
All width and no depth.
Driven by the fear of missing out,
we're constantly plugging in to our devices
at the expense of real relationships and passions.
Make the technology work for you,
find your passions and explore them.

'Passion is universal humanity. Without it religion,
history, romance and art would be useless.'
Honoré de Balzac (1799-1850)

Build the foundations

Too often we jump in before we do any homework.
We start projects or make commitments –
without mastering the essentials or
doing basic research;
without assessing risks or gathering necessary tools.
Take the time to build a solid base.
It will save lots of heartache.

'The loftier the building, the deeper must the foundation be laid.'
Thomas a Kempis (1380-1471)

Add value

Always strive to leave things better
than you found them.
Make this a central theme in your approach to life.
It will set you apart from those
satisfied with the status quo;
from those who surf along with the crowd;
and those who lack the imagination
to aim for greatness.

'How wonderful it is that nobody need wait a single
moment before starting to improve the world.'
Anne Frank (1929-1945)

Seek the truth

It's our brightest beacon.
It lights a clear path.
It illuminates the goal.
It exposes the obstacles and deceptions.
It simplifies life.

'Always do right. This will gratify some people and astonish the rest.'
Mark Twain (Samuel Langhorne Clemens) (1835-1910)

You are your competition

Don't be distracted by judging yourself against others.
Set your own standards.
Judge yourself against those standards.
Do it honestly and without delusion.
Accept your verdict and move on.

'I am the master of my fate; I am the captain of my soul.'
William Ernest Henley (1849-1903), 'Invictus'

Share your smile

It radiates light.
It reflects your inner warmth.
It engenders confidence.
It eases tensions.
It opens doors.
It's contagious.

'Those who bring sunshine to the lives of others
cannot keep it from themselves.'

J. M. Barrie (1860-1937)

Never give in

Persistence often pays unexpected dividends.
By staying the course you open up possibilities.
You ask rewarding questions of yourself ...
and the challenges you face.
You find unexplored paths.
And you reveal your inner strength.

'It is not enough that we do our best; sometimes
we must do what is required.'

Sir Winston Churchill (1874-1965)

Rewrite

Always consider your first attempt as a draft:
whether it's a speech, a letter, a
presentation or a novel.
Even the greatest authors and orators take this view.
They lay down their thoughts in their initial work.
They re-think, refine and polish.
It's like focusing your lens until your subject is sharp.

The first draft of anything is shit.'

Ernest Hemingway (1899-1961)

Speak up

But only when you have something worthwhile to say.
Until then, listen and evaluate.
Resist the urge to respond just
to show your knowledge.
Wait until you can add to the situation.
But when you have a view and you believe in it,
speak up.
Speak out ... and mean it.

'The less you talk the more you're listened to.'
Abigail van Buren (Pauline Esther Phillips) (1918-2013)

Walk away from regret

Regret can be a heavy burden:
a mournful millstone that weighs you down.
It will blur your focus and turn your mind back ...
like endlessly replaying a ghostly movie.
Look to the future, free from the gloom.
Seek the light and walk towards it.

'Never look back unless you are planning to go that way.'
Henry David Thoreau (1817-1862)

Focus on the possible

Don't be distracted by the problems, the negatives.
Don't give them more weight than they deserve.
Break down the task into manageable elements.
Deal first with what you can resolve.
You'll gain the confidence, perspective and strength
to challenge more difficult obstacles.

'The Possible's slow fuse is lit by the imagination.'
Emily Dickinson (1830-1886)

You are not your mistakes

Treat your mistakes as lessons not sentences.
Don't allow them to define who you are.
Consider why you made them.
Learn from them.
Emerge stronger.
Resolve not to repeat them.
Move ahead.

'Experience is simply the name we give our mistakes.'
Oscar Wilde (1854-1900)

Become a conduit

Be a connector.
But be a discerning connector.
Add meaning to your connections.
The more you help others, the more
you will benefit yourself.
Avoid the hyper-connectivity of
mindless social networking.
Instead, prefer intelligent, selective
mutually-beneficial links.

'Listen to many, speak to a few.'
William Shakespeare (1564-1616), 'Hamlet'

Stand your ground

When you know in your heart that you're right.
When abandoning your view is the easy way out.
Double-check your position.
If satisfied, gather your courage and stand firm.
It's not stubborn to maintain your beliefs:
It's a show of your character.

'Our lives begin to end the day we become
silent about things that matter.'

Martin Luther King Jr (1929-1968)

Choose your mentors wisely

Good mentors are one of life's finest gifts.
But one size doesn't fit all.
Use your intelligence, your experience
and your common sense:
choose a mentor with wisdom, compassion and vision.
Great achievers aren't necessarily great teachers.
Look for someone you respect,
someone who will inspire.

'I am not a teacher, but an awakener.'

Robert Frost (1874-1963)

Embrace accountability

It's too easy to accept life's successes as good luck.
They encourage you to see the failures as bad luck.
Take the time to differentiate.
Enjoy the achievements you've gained from hard work.
But take responsibility for your negative actions.
That way you'll always sleep soundly.

'Shallow men believe in luck.'

Ralph Waldo Emerson (1803-1882)

Distil your dreams

It's great to have big dreams.
They can buoy you through dark times.
And inspire you to reach for the stars.
But sometimes it's worth focusing on
smaller parts of your dreams.
These can often be attainable in the shorter term.
And can underwrite your longer expeditions.

'All that we see or seem is but a dream within a dream.'
Edgar Allan Poe (1809-1849)

Stop labelling

The media is obsessed with labels:
always searching for a one-word
summary of people's lives.
Resist the temptation to join in.
Keep an open mind about individuals.
They're almost always more interesting
than their labels.
Give them a chance to be a genuine individual.

'Labels are for filing. Labels are for clothing.
Labels are not for people.'

Martina Navratilova (1956-)

Value your loved ones

It seems so obvious.
But how often do we take our
dearest ones for granted?
Remember how they have supported us
at times when nobody else would.
Think of how they form part of the fabric of our lives.
Take time to tell them how much you love them.
Treasure the time you have with them.

'Remember that wherever your heart is,
there you will find your treasure.'

Paulo Coelho (1947-), 'The Alchemist'

Never stand still

The only constant in our lives is change.
You can try to fight it ... but change doesn't care.
It will remorselessly grind on,
whether you like it or not.
Make sure you're looking forward.
Be adaptable: make change work for you.
If you're marking time, you're going backward.

'The systems that fail are those that rely on the permanency of
human nature, and not on its growth and development.'
Oscar Wilde (1854-1900), 'The Soul of Man under Socialism'

You get what you work for

There are exceptions, but hard work
usually brings rewards.
Like sporting pros, the harder you work,
the luckier you get.
Position yourself for your best chance at success.
Should circumstances turn against you
take satisfaction in knowing you tried your best.
That's way ahead of leaving things to chance.

'Amateurs practise until they get it right, professionals
practise until they can't get it wrong.'

Anonymous

Find the humour

Whatever the situation,
however dire it seems at first glance,
there's always a bright side.
And looking at the funny side releases tensions.
It puts things into perspective,
and opens the mind to possible solutions.

'Humour is one of the best ingredients of survival.'
Aung San Suu Kyi (1945-)

Make your presence felt

You only get one chance at this life.
It makes no sense then, to simply
disappear into the crowd.
Pay due respect to your existence.
Acknowledge those who helped to form you.
Isolate the things that are precious to you.
Stand up for them. Live them.

'To believe in something and not to live it is dishonest.'
Mohandas Karamchand (Mahatma) Gandhi (1869-1948)

Know what you want

How often do we just meander through life?
Wandering without any real purpose ...
or worse, allowing others to set our agendas.
Take some time to focus on your real priorities.
Distil your goals and choose your path towards them.
It's the shortest distance between
desire and fulfilment.

'When you know better, you do better.'

Maya Angelou (1928-)

Don't wait for perfect

Seeking the perfect start can paralyse you.
It's far better to make a start, to get underway.
Then make adjustments, or rewrite as you proceed.
Once you've started, options will present themselves.
And creativity will flow from the process.

'Have no fear of perfection – you'll never reach it.'
Salvador Dali (1904-1989)

Look with wide eyes

Our world increasingly favours specialists.
They tend to view things through a close-up lens.
They become experts and focus on minutiae.
While they increase our knowledge,
they narrow our horizons.
Choose the wide-angled view.
There lies perspective.
And unlimited horizons.

'The responsibility of tolerance lies with
those who have the wider vision.'

George Eliot (Mary Anne Evans) (1819-1880)

Lose the excuses

Be honest with yourself about your cop-outs.
In your heart you know when
they're becoming crutches.
When you're tempted to say you don't have time,
reschedule to make some.
When you're about to place the blame
on others, reflect first.
Where you can influence the result ... do so.

'When you blame others, you give up your power to change.'
Douglas Adams (1952-2001)

Design your own future

You can wait passively for your future to unfold,
or you can take the initiative and create your own.
Sure, there will be many things you can't control.
But, there will be many more, over
which you have power.
At the very least, play a leading role.
Plan the future of your dreams.

'Life isn't about finding yourself. Life is about creating yourself.'
George Bernard Shaw (1856-1950)

Do it now

It's always easier to put things off until later.
But it usually compounds the problems.
And it magnifies their impact when they finally arrive.
Grasp the chance, take action now.
It brings great satisfaction.
And offers many unexpected opportunities.

The future depends on what you do today.'
Mohandas Karamchand (Mahatma) Gandhi (1869-1948)

Chart your own course

Being yourself doesn't mean being selfish.
It means discovering the truths at your core,
and being comfortable in your own skin.
It's living according to your central truths.
Not being swayed by the vagaries of the herd,
but having the courage to follow your heart.

'Be yourself, everyone else is taken.'

Oscar Wilde (1854-1900)

Be eternally curious

Perhaps the most valuable trait of all is curiosity.
It nurtures hope and optimism.
It inspires invention.
It nourishes intelligence and drives progress.
Encourage it.
Embrace its flow and share its rewards.

'I have no special talents. I am only passionately curious.'
Albert Einstein (1879-1955)

Focus on the facts,
not the messenger

It's too easy to lash out at the messenger.
Instead, look behind them:
separate the message from the messenger.
Weigh the merits, not the personalities.
It will save you from many emotional traps.

'Don't kill the messenger.'

Sophocles (496BC-406BC) Antigone

We're all entrepreneurs

We can't all be Steve Jobs or Sir Richard Branson ...
but we can all build our own livelihoods.
We can strive for self-reliance.
Learn from the brilliant ones,
observe their methods and structures.
Mould them to your circumstances and needs.

'Make the most of yourself – for that is all there is of you.'
Ralph Waldo Emerson (1803-1882)

Enlist help

It's tempting to try to do everything yourself.
But it's dopey.
Even Einstein called on other minds to expand his.
When you think you have all the skills
to complete the task, seek complementary
skills and the fresh eyes of others.
You'll pay them respect and unleash potential.

'I not only use all the brains I have, but all I can borrow.'
Woodrow Wilson (1856-1924)

Above all, be genuine

We're surrounded by artifice, half-truths & advertising.
Every day we meet people without
a shred of substance.
Many of them are vastly successful – and famous.
But they don't last the distance.
Join those who mean what they say
and say what they mean.
They are the people who leave their mark.

'If you tell the truth, you don't have to remember anything.'
Mark Twain (Samuel Langhorne Clemens) (1835-1910)

Plan to live, not retire

Retirement is an unfortunate word.
It implies a resignation from active participation in life.
Take a different viewpoint.
Consider your life as an evolving, continually
enriching experience.
Celebrate the wisdom born of your experiences.
Use that wisdom to constantly grow at
a pace of your choosing.

'Live as if you were to die tomorrow. Learn
as if you were to live forever.'
Mohandas Karamchand (Mahatma) Gandhi (1869-1948)

Make the most of you

Concentrate on your strengths

Most of the world's great achievers have done this.
Don't waste energy worrying about your weaknesses.
Hone your strong points.
Master them and allow them to flourish.
They will spark your passion,
and inspire you to greater heights.

'Passion is in all great searches and is necessary
to all creative endeavours.'

W. Eugene Smith (1918-1978)

You are not a brand

Ignore the marketeers and the social media gurus.
You're a person: a unique, shining, complex individual.
You can do so many things they don't realise.
Don't let them fence you in.
Don't be boxed and labelled.
Seek the freedom of the unencumbered individual.

'You have to be unique and different and shine in your own way.'
Lady Gaga (Stefani Joanne Angelina Germanotta) (1986-)

Wear the scars proudly

Take real satisfaction from your hard-won lessons.
You have earned the wisdom they brought.
Don't take it for granted.
If you didn't have the courage to take the risks,
you wouldn't have reaped the rewards.
Take pride in your experience.

'Turn your wounds into wisdom'

Oprah Winfrey (1954-)

Money doesn't equal happiness

There's no doubt lack of money can make life harder.
Money can bring power, it can give you options.
But financial success does not guarantee happiness.
Your happiness still lies with your
choices and your actions.
At the end, all you're left with is love and memories.
You won't be counting your money then.

'True wealth is the ability to fully experience life.'
Henry David Thoreau (1817-1862)

Appreciate your achievements

Good leaders always praise their team's achievements.
Recognition signals appreciation
and fosters renewed effort.
Give yourself some credit where it is due.
There'll be plenty ready to talk your work down.
Take a moment to acknowledge your successes.
And build a little self-confidence.

'Self-reverence, self-knowledge and self-control:
these three alone lead life to sovereign power.'
Alfred Lord Tennyson (1809-1892)

Widen your horizons

Most of us are city-bound:
physically, mentally and spiritually.
We're hemmed in by artificial boundaries.
And restricted by customs and regulations.
Seek inspiration outside your fences.
Take the overview.

'Vision is the art of seeing what is invisible to others.'
Jonathan Swift (1667-1745)

Listen without judging

Are you really listening or just waiting to talk?
Trust your intellect, open your mind.
Don't prefabricate your responses,
Don't try to showcase your wit.
Listen and respond in the moment.
You'll be surprised at how much more you'll learn.

'When people talk, listen completely. Most people never listen.'
Ernest Hemingway (1899-1961)

Go to the heart of problems

Peel away the wrappings and find
the core of the problem.
You may need to break it down,
or to take the problem out of its environment.
You may need to change your viewpoint.
When you find the essence,
you often simplify things.

'Inside every large problem is a small
problem struggling to be freed.'

Anonymous

It's usually about focus

If you examine the real achievers ...
... in life, in the arts, in sports, in business ...
they're usually the ones with unwavering focus.
Indeed, focus is often the only difference
between competitors.
Consider how well you focus on the main task.
Filter out the distractions, watch the difference.

'To follow, without halt, one aim: there is the secret of success.'
Anna Pavlova (1881-1931)

Savour the beauty

Look for the beauty in all you see and do.
It will inspire and sustain you.
It will make sense of so many puzzles.
It's not always obvious.
It's often obscured.
But it always brings you closer to the truth.

'If something is not beautiful, it is probably not true.'
John Keats (1795-1821)

Unleash the song

We all have the makings of a wonderful song inside us.
If only we allow it to flourish.
It's a song built on the joy we often lock inside us.
It's based on the melodies of our lives.
Unleash your inner music.
Give it a chance to burst out.

'The mass of men lead lives of quiet desperation
and die with the song still in them.'

Henry David Thoreau (1817-1862)

Value your honour

You can't underestimate the impact of honour.
It gives your life a solid structure.
It aligns your heart to your mind.
It gives confidence to those who deal with you.
It simplifies decisions.
Wear it with pride.

'Mine honour is my life; both grow into one:
take honour from me, and my life is done.'
William Shakespeare (1864-1616), 'Richard II'

Be succinct

Present your arguments like a fine reduction sauce.
Distil, rethink and rework.
Eliminate the padding.
Refine your ideas to their essence.
Their force will be magnified tenfold.

'Simplicity is the ultimate sophistication.'
Leonardo da Vinci (1452-1519)

Do not assume

On all the important issues, double-check your facts.
Don't assume someone has already checked them.
That's taking the easy way out every time.
And it's fraught with danger.
Assumption is the root cause of most disasters.
Satisfy yourself before you act.

'Few are those who see with their own eyes
and feel with their own hearts.'

Albert Einstein (1879-1955)

You are strong

Your strength will surprise you.
Most of us have an inner, untapped
high-tensile strength.
It's there when you most need it.
It will enable you to rise above your challenges.
Allow yourself to trust it.
Call on it with confidence.

'We acquire the strength we overcome.'
Ralph Waldo Emerson (1803-1882)

Do it now

Genuine opportunities are rare.
And they often come when we're engrossed elsewhere.
Learn to keep your antenna tuned for them.
Have an open mind, consider the possibilities.
Assess the chance against your experience.
If it holds up, take it.

'Opportunity is missed by most people because
it is dressed in overalls and looks like work.'
Thomas Edison (1847-1931)

Give credit where it's due

The temptation is to appropriate others'
ideas as our own.
Or to minimise their influence on us ...
as though that somehow makes us
stronger or more original.
We are all products of our experiences with others.
Acknowledge those who have helped
form you and your beliefs.
It repays their gifts and enriches your soul.

'When eating a fruit, think of the person who planted the tree.'
Vietnamese proverb

There are no shortcuts

You can pay your dues first.
Or you can experience great advances ...
and then have to pay your dues.
Either way, there are no real shortcuts.
The rich experience you gain as you learn,
pays off many times over in the long run.

'Good judgement comes from experience and
a lot of that comes from bad judgement.'

Will Rogers (1879-1935)

Make your time count

It's our most valuable asset, treat it with respect.
Don't take the future for granted.
Our time is finite and it's sought after.
Enjoy the present.
Savour every precious moment.
Spend your time wisely.

'Time is the wisest counsellor of all.'

Seneca (4BC-65AD)

Share your vision

Don't hide your great visions,
Or work to reach them in a vacuum.
Tell others of your dream.
Inspire them to join you on your quest.
It will widen your pool of wisdom,
And underpin your determination.

'Every time you share your vision, you strengthen your
own subconscious belief that you can achieve it.'

Jack Canfield (1944-)

Work to a plan

Follow your strategy, not your moods.
That way, you can ride the emotional waves,
and still make progress towards your goal.
Accept your feelings, take note of them,
but don't allow them to derail the journey.
Ride the upswings,
push through the downswings.

'Don't judge each day by the harvest you reap
but by the seeds that you plant.'

Robert Louis Stevenson (1850-1894)

Think like an explorer

Be the pioneer in thought, not the camp follower.
Seek new tracks.
Imagine new paths.
Challenge old ideas and ways.
Be prepared to backtrack from dead-ends.
Aspire to original views.

'One who walks in another's tracks leaves no footprints.'
Italian Proverb

Dress the part

It doesn't mean dressing to conform
or to please others.
Or worse, to mindlessly follow a fad.
Rather, dress for your purpose, in your style:
for comfort, respect, protection, climate.
Seek elegance and make a statement for the occasion.
It will bring you confidence and respect from others.

'Language is the dress of thought.'

Samuel Johnson (1709-1784)

Make the most of you

Work with joy

The older you get, the more you appreciate life.
The old line is right: life is too short.
It's too short to be lived without joy.
Find joy in your work, or find other work.
It can be in the unlikeliest places.
But without it, life is hollow.

'The happiness of your life depends upon
the quality of your thoughts.'

Marcus Aurelius (121-180)

Seek change from within

It's laudable to try to change the world.
But sometimes we choose the wrong starting point.
Start by looking within.
See if the problem is rooted within you,
If so, that's where the change should begin.
Then your commitment will be unshakeable.

'Everyone thinks of changing the world but
no one thinks of changing himself.'

Leo Tolstoy (1828-1910)

Get a pet

When you need time to reflect, play with your pet.
It will connect you to nature.
And put your stresses on pause.
It will renew your spirit.
And allow you to recalibrate your emotions.
It will remind you about unconditional love.

'A dog is the only thing on earth that loves
you more than he loves himself.'
Josh Billings (Henry Wheeler Shaw) (1818-1885)

Ignore the naysayers

Fault-finders swarm like mosquitoes.
They delight in bringing you down.
They live under a black cloud,
and want to cast their shadow over you too.
Seek the light,
leave them behind.
Outshine them.

'I don't think of all the misery but of the beauty that still remains.'
Anne Frank (1929-1945)

Push the boundaries

Genuinely inventive ideas usually arrive unheralded.
In fact, many look ridiculous.
Others are shrouded in confusion.
And tossed aside by so-called experts.
Until they are tested.
Then their true merit shines through.

'If at first an idea does not sound absurd,
then there is no hope for it.'

Albert Einstein (1879-1955)

Be the exception

Don't be part of a cover band: write original material.
Don't blend in with the crowd or
camouflage your abilities.
Be proud of your achievements, hone your skills.
Back yourself.
Trust your judgement.
Take the lead.

'How glorious it is – and also how painful – to be an exception.'
Alfred de Musset (1810-1857)

Choose your words

Observe how lazy many are with their speech.
Separate yourself from the mob: speak with precision.
Read voraciously, study the masters.
Listen intently to the great orators.
Learn their patterns, discern their structures.
Use your words to their full potential.

'Words are, of course, the most powerful drug used by mankind.'
Rudyard Kipling (1816-1936)

Avoid the noise

We live and work with a cacophony
that's often overwhelming.
It dulls our senses and drowns out ideas.
White noise obscures issues and individuals.
Don't waste your time yelling into the noise.
Seek the silent moments.
Then speak with conviction.

'The silent man is the best to listen to.'

Japanese proverb

Ask yourself the hard questions

What could you yet be?
What holds you back?
What do you fear?
Where is your love?
What gives you hope?
How will you be remembered?

'There are no foolish questions, and no man becomes
foolish until he has stopped asking questions.'
Charles Proteus Steinmetz (1865-1923)

Seek out the wise ones

Don't confuse knowledge with wisdom.
Watch for the observers:
those with wise heads and hearts.
They know the rules ... and the exceptions.
They take the long view, the rounded view.
Grasp the chance to spend time with them.

'A single conversation with a wise man is
better than ten years of study.'

Chinese proverb

Travel

Travel as often as your life allows.
Some chances only present themselves once.
See yourself and your life against
an unfamiliar backdrop.
It will throw them into focus.
It will bring you perspective.
It will bring you wisdom.

'The whole object of travel is not to set foot on foreign land; it is
at last to set foot on one's own country as a foreign land.'
G. K. Chesterton (1874-1936)

Write a diary or journal

Do it for three months.
Keep it private so you can be totally honest.
Record your thoughts, impressions and feelings.
After three months, review your work.
See what it teaches you about your true inner feelings.
What changes should you make to your life?

'Every man's memory is his private literature.'
Aldous Huxley (1864-1963)

Do what you love

You'll attract like-minded friends,
partners and workmates.
You'll create a harmonious workplace.
You'll light the creative fuse.
And ignite passions.
The alchemy produces unexpected results.
And maintains enthusiasm.

'Nothing great was ever achieved without enthusiasm.'
Ralph Waldo Emerson (1803-1882)

Make a creative space

Give yourself the best chance to be creative.
Find a place of solitude:
somewhere you can put your mind on 'pause'.
Remove all mundane reminders: bills, emails, etc
Make this your retreat ...
a place where you can stand apart from the world.

'Imagination is the highest kite one can fly.'

Anonymous

Fail better

Consider failures as lessons,
steps towards ultimate success.
Don't take them personally.
You may have failed: you are not a failure.
Turn the setback into feedback.
Make sure you fail forward, not backward.

'I have not failed. I've just found 10,000 ways that won't work.'
Thomas Edison (1847-1931)

Pause for thought

Don't rush to respond ...
especially if you're angry or frustrated.
Whether replying to an email, or to an accusation ...
reflect, even sleep on it, before reacting.
It can save you endless trouble.
It can open up unconsidered opportunities.

'Never miss a good chance to shut up.'

Will Rogers (1879-1935)

Share your problems

A problem shared can be a problem divided.
But carefully choose your confidante.
Make sure of their trust.
Draw on their experience and their wisdom.
View things through new eyes.
Shine new light on your problem.

'Someone to tell it to is one of the fundamental
needs of human beings.'

Miles Franklin (1879-1954)

Chose your battles carefully

Some battles are simply not worth the energy.
And can leave both sides as losers.
Make sure your battles are big enough
to be worth fighting,
yet small enough for you to win them.
If you can otherwise resolve the issues ...
seriously consider it.

'War doesn't determine who is right, only who is left.'
Bertrand Russell (1872-1970)

Keep your mind open

It's too easy to fall back on your prejudices.
Instead, look at important issues through fresh eyes.
Challenge your entrenched opinions.
Consider things from others' perspectives.
It may reinforce your position.
But it may provoke a new approach.

'Loyalty to a petrified opinion never yet broke
a chain or freed a human soul.'
Mark Twain (Samuel Langhorne Clemens) (1835-1910)

Change perspective

Our problems depend so much on our preconceptions.
Many are shaped by our viewpoint.
Changing our view will cause some to disappear,
and reveal solutions for others.
The mystery is often in our mindset,
and vanishes as we shift our perspective.

'Wearing leather just on the soles of my shoes
is equivalent to covering the earth with it.'

Shantideva (around 685-763)

Dream by day

Allow yourself to visualise your dreams.
Implant them in the back of your mind.
You'll gradually gravitate towards them.
Subconsciously your decisions will find the paths.
Often, even before you're aware of it.
Then those dreams will be within reach.

'The eye sees only what the mind is prepared to comprehend.'
Henri-Louis Bergson (1859-1941)

Deliver the message

Don't assume your message has been received,
just because you've sent it.
People often give you the answer they think you want.
It's easy to assume that's what they believe.
Make sure they have understood.
Double-check their response.

'The single biggest problem with communication
is the illusion that it has occurred.'

George Bernard Shaw (1856-1950)

Make the time

If you wait until you have the time,
You'll never get anything done.
Life has a way of filling in available time.
If you have something that must be done,
You'll have to make the time for it.
If it's important enough, just do it.

'You will never find the time for anything. You must make it.'
Charles Buxton (1823-1871)

Lose the baggage

Whether taking a voyage or moving through life,
only take the essentials.
Heavy baggage will slow your journey.
And make you less flexible.
Travel light. Enjoy the scenery.
Focus on your experiences.

'He who would travel happily must travel light.'
Antoine de Saint-Exupery (1900-1944)

Take the lead

Sometimes you know it's up to you.
You're the logical person to lead the way.
Sometimes, fear or modesty prevents you.
But you'll know when the time is right.
Ignore the fear: it will evaporate.
Take command,
follow your instincts.

'A Leader is a dealer in hope.'

Napoleon Bonaparte (1769-1821)

Know what you want

Easy to say: not so easy to achieve.
Be honest with yourself.
Think deeply about your true goals.
Question your motivations.
Isolate your essential aims.
Decide on your course.

'It's not what you look at that matters; it's what you see.'
Henry David Thoreau (1817-1862)

Lift your energy level

The great ones can do it, no matter
how exhausted they are.
It's what sets the sporting champions apart.
They have the ability to rise to the occasion.
They can manage their energy.
And draw on it when they need it most.
It's an invaluable asset.

'The human body is a machine which winds its own wings.'
Julien de la Mettrie (1709-1751), 'L'Homme Machine'

Declutter

We are awash with unnecessary possessions.
We collect them daily.
They weigh us down and distract us.
Take the time to rid yourself of needless junk.
You'll be surprised how liberating it is.
You'll be delighted at the clarity it offers.

'Life is really simple, but we insist on making it complicated.'
Confucius (551BC-479BC)

Get fit

You don't have to become an elite sportsperson.
But you must respect your body and guard your health.
Find a routine that balances nutrition and exercise.
Tailor it to your lifestyle and to your stage in life.
Embrace it.
Stick to it.

'If I'd known I was going to live this long, I would
have taken better care of myself.'

Anonymous

Celebrate

Don't be so focused on achieving things ...
that you forget to celebrate when you reach your goals.
Don't immediately refocus on the next target.
Take the time to enjoy success and reinvigorate.
Savour the taste of the achievement.
Use the recollection to spur you to greater heights.

'There is only one success – to be able to
spend your life in your own way.'

Christopher Morley (1890-1957)

Learn from the best

If you want to be great, study how the greats do it.
Seek out the finest exponents in your field.
Learn about them: their back stories, their challenges.
Dissect their approaches.
Understand their rationales.
Build on their achievements.

'The important thing is not to stop questioning.'
Albert Einstein (1879-1955)

Give yourself

You can give your money.
You can give your possessions.
But the greatest gift you can give is yourself.
If you give from the heart
you enrich yourself as much as the recipient.

'The only gift is a portion of yourself.'
Ralph Waldo Emerson (1803-1882)

Make the most of you

Seek wisdom

Wherever you are, whatever you're doing, aim to learn.
Make it second-nature.
Try to learn something valuable every day.
It doesn't have to be profound.
But make it useful.
Add it to the reservoir of wisdom from which you live.

'Wisdom outweighs any wealth.'

Sophocles (496BC-406BC)

Turn fear into growth

Fear can be a valuable asset.
Challenge it. Look it in the eye.
Turn it into a lesson.
When we overcome fear we take ownership of it.
We convert it into an achievement.
And step up over it.

'To conquer fear is the beginning of wisdom'
Bertrand Russell (1872-1970)

Embrace your freedom

In a world in which so many are enslaved:
by politics, or finances, or health,
we should appreciate our freedoms.
We should never take them for granted.
We should guard them ...
and do our best to extend them to others.

'Let freedom never perish in your hands.'

Joseph Addison (1672-1719)

Enjoy your home

Your house should be your home,
not just somewhere you sleep.
It's where your spirit lives ...
where your family loves and understands you.
It's where you come for renewal.
It's your haven.
It's where you're never alone.

'There is nothing like staying at home for real comfort.'
Jane Austen (1775-1817)

Contribute

Whatever you're doing, add your touch to it.
Be active, not passive.
If you can't take the lead, support others.
Don't seek praise.
Do it for the satisfaction of being part of the team:
the glow of a job well done.

'Gettin' good players is easy. Gettin' 'em to
play together is the hard part.'

Casey Stengel (1890-1975)

Take your chance

Opportunities are rarely missed.
If you let them go by, someone else will grab them.
Don't allow fear to immobilise you
Learn to recognize the potential
Open your mind to the possibilities.
Seize opportunity when it beckons.

'In Chinese the word 'crisis' is composed of two characters: one represents danger and the other represents opportunity.'
John Fitzgerald Kennedy (1917-1963)

Make the most of you

Enjoy today

It's not complicated:
we have no guarantees for the future;
we can't rewind the past;
we must live in the present.
Use the past for wisdom ...
and the future for inspiration.
Live now!

'Nothing is worth more than this day.'
Johann Wolfgang von Goethe (1749-1832)

Make anger work for you

You can let anger paralyse you into furious inaction.
You can waste precious time plotting vengeance.
Or you can use your anger positively.
Pause, reflect, take control of the passion.
Draw strength from it.
Respond with intelligence.

'You will not be punished for your anger,
you will punished by your anger.'
Gautama Buddha (around 563BC-483BC)

Look for meaning

Often you won't find it,
but seeking meaning in your life will sustain you.
Finding meaning makes things more palatable.
Even seeking it can make them tolerable.
When things reveal themselves to you,
wondrous doors open.

'He who has a Why can bear almost any How.'
Friedrich Nietzsche (1844-1900)

Reject resentment

Wallowing in resentment is absurd.
It's like punishing yourself ...
and expecting someone else to suffer.
If someone forces you to hold a grudge,
then they've conquered you.
Don't let resentment get between you and living.

'Malice drinks one half of its own poison.'

Seneca (4BC-65AD)

Cherish goodwill

In our often-cynical world, goodwill is a treasure.
It brings light to dark moments.
It enables collaboration,
and leads to great achievements.
Bring goodwill to your dealings.
Trust others unless they betray your trust.
Open the possibilities.

'Attitude is a little thing that makes a big difference.'
Winston Churchill (1874-1965)

Astonish them

Always set your aims high ...
so high that you'll amaze people.
Make it your default position.
Even when you fall short, you'll impress.
And when you reach your target ...
you'll leave them astounded!

'It's not the mountain we conquer but ourselves.'
Edmund Hillary (1919-2008)

Seek solitude

Never stop looking for insight and understanding
in the world around you ...
in the people you meet ...
in the lessons you learn.
Whatever your age ...
you stay young when you're learning.

'Nowhere can man find a quieter or more untroubled
retreat than in his own soul.'

Marcus Aurelius (121AD-180AD)

Seek insight

Our world pushes us towards shallowness.
All width and no depth.
Driven by the fear of missing out,
we're constantly plugging in to our devices
at the expense of real relationships and passions.
Make the technology work for you,
find your passions and explore them.

'I don't think much of a man who is not wiser
today than he was yesterday.'

Abraham Lincoln (1809-1865)

Adjust

Nothing in our world remains static.
It's either growing or declining.
Unless you adjust to the changes, you'll stultify.
Treat change as an opportunity to refresh.
The longer you resist, the greater the shock.
Adjust gradually.

'They must often change, who would be
constant in happiness or wisdom.'

Confucius (551BC-479BC)

Forgive yourself

Many see forgiveness as weakness.
On the contrary it's a sign of real strength.
It won't change the past.
But it will improve the future.
While we should forgive others,
we should also remember to forgive ourselves.
That way all the baggage is jettisoned.

'The weak can never forgive. Forgiveness
is the attribute of the strong.'
Mohandas Karamchand (Mahatma) Gandhi (1869-1948)

Give compliments

They take such little effort.
Yet bring so much joy.
When you're impressed ...
take the time to acknowledge it.
It will make someone's day.
It will lift your spirits too.

'I can live for two months on a good compliment.'
Mark Twain (Samuel Langhorne Clemens) (1835-1910)

Embrace good manners

They are such a civilising force.
They pay respect to others.
They reveal your sincerity and character.
Indeed, they reveal your strength ...
as rudeness is a sure sign of weakness.

'Life be not so short but that there is always time for courtesy.'
Ralph Waldo Emerson (1803-1882)

Be Punctual

Punctuality is one of the most
admirable of basic courtesies.
It shows you value others' time as much as your own.
It is also very practical:
it enables meetings to start and end on time;
it engenders respect.

'You may delay, but time will not.'

Benjamin Franklin (1706-1790)

Be a team player

It's so rewarding to be part of a successful team.
It's central to success at any level.
It's the essence of mateship:
an amalgam of individuals caring for each other,
and working in harmony.
Even if you're the leader, be part of the team.

'Remember upon the conduct of each depends the fate of all.'
Alexander the Great (356BC-323BC)

Be there

The importance of being fully present sounds obvious.
But in our maelstrom of bewildering change,
it's easy to wander mentally and emotionally.
Being there allows us to fully participate in our lives,
not be just a casual observer,
always focused on some future notion.

'The living moment is everything.'

D.H. Lawrence (1885-1930)

Learn to sell

Like it or not, we all work in sales.
We must let others know about our skills.
We must take our work to the market.
It's not about ego:
it's about visibility in a kaleidoscope of offerings.

'I'm a travelling salesman. I deal in ideas.'
Martin Kippenberger (1953-1997)

Learn from success

We tend to look for lessons from failure,
but to accept our successes without critique.
Examine your triumphs as you would your disasters.
Seek wisdom from them.
Find the common threads,
try to replicate them.

'Always walk through life as though you have
something new to learn and you will.'

Vernon Howard (1918-1992)

Spread your risks

Daring is central to following your passions,
and living life to the full.
But temper your risk-taking whenever you can.
Think like a good gambler and bet each way.
Use your experience to assess the dangers.
And make a sensible choice.

'Luck never gives, it only lends.'

Swedish proverb

Consider first impressions

How often we judge by that first meeting.
And often that memory is indelible.
If you're looking to impress, bear that in mind.
Think ahead. Learn about your companions.
Be true to yourself and your character.

'Pleasure is the flower that passes; remembrance,
the lasting perfume.'
Stanislaus-Jean, chevalier de Boufflers (1738-1815)

Make personal contact

The digital world thrives on isolation.
Use it where it can bring you benefits,
but make sure you retain the personal touch.
Value the subtleties of face-to-face conversations ...
the magic of eye contact,
the warmth of human touch.

'The eyes show the strength of your soul.'

Paul Coelho (1947-)

Read voraciously

No matter whether it's pbooks, ebooks or online,
expose your mind to great writing.
It can transform and transport you.
It can send your sprits soaring,
and replenish your soul.
It will constantly widen your horizons.

'A book has but one voice but it does not instruct everyone alike.'
Thomas a Kempis (1380-1471)

Blaze your own trail

Learn from those who have gone before you.
But don't follow their path slavishly.
Maintain your individuality.
Add your own skills and experiences.
Make your own choices.

'Don't try to be your predecessor.'

Arnaud Nourry (1961-)

Wake with the sun

Try to sync your rhythms to nature.
Rising with the dawn brings a special energy.
It kickstarts your day.
and gives you the momentum to drive on.
Draw power from the warmth and the light.

'Lose an hour in the morning and you will be all day hunting for it.'
Richard Whately (1787-1863)

Seek feedback

Most of us are happy to give advice when asked.
And we do so in the spirit of goodwill,
aiming to use our experience to help and to guide.
So never fear asking for advice.
Just make sure you respect the source,
then use it wisely.

'It is more easy to be wise for others than for ourselves.'
Francois Duc de la Rochefoucauld (1613-1680)

Hone your speaking skills

Above all, know what you're speaking about.
Be genuine, allow your passion to shine through.
Watch and learn from the great orators.
See how they make contact with their audience:
with their eyes and the tone of their voice.
Then practise, practise.

'Be sincere; be brief; be seated.'
Franklin Delano Roosevelt (1882-1945)

Meditate

If possible, learn the art properly.
If not, create your own form of meditation.
Teach yourself to find the wonder of the child ...
as you allow your mind to settle into calmness.
Where there is chaos and conflict about you,
turn your mind into a silent haven,
without judgement.

'We live in a world starved for solitude, silence, and private:
and therefore starved for meditation and true friendship.'
C. S. Lewis (1898-1963)

Get a good chair

It may not seem important,
but it's a vital ingredient for your health and creativity.
A good chair can transform your working day,
especially if your work keeps you at a desk for hours.
Check with an expert.
Find your most appropriate chair.
Invest in it.

'A chair is a very difficult object. A skyscraper is almost
easier. That is why Chippendale is famous.'
Ludwig Mies van der Rohe (1886-1969)

Eat well

Think about what you're putting into your body.
Keep it simple: as unprocessed as possible.
and organic if practical.
Try for overall balance.
Try not to overeat.
A good general rule:
if it's packaged and has a mascot, avoid it!

'Eat little, sleep sound.'

Iranian proverb

Beware of gurus

And life coaches.
In the end, you're the captain of your ship.
Steer your own course.
Learn from others …
but make sure they're worthy of emulation.
Just because they claim expertise,
doesn't mean they have it.

'Of course, I talk to myself … sometimes I need expert advice!'
Anonymous

Help others

No activity gives more satisfaction.
It liberates: it hints at our higher purpose.
It brings us all closer together.
When you think 'someone should do something':
you are the someone.
However small, however insignificant it may seem,
it does make a difference.

'Help one person at a time and always start
with the person nearest you.'
Mother Teresa (Anjeze Gonxhe Bojaxhiu) (1910-1997)

Keep your mind active

Like your body, if you don't use your mind, you'll lose it.
So treat your mind with the same respect as your body.
Exercise it, rest it, expand its capacity.
Read, meditate, question, challenge.
Do puzzles.
Learn a language.
Push your mental boundaries.

'If only I may grow: firmer, simpler, quieter, warmer.'
Dag Hammarskjold (1905-1961)

Reach for clarity

Push on through the storm of information around you.
See through the confusion and conflicts.
Learn to distil and reveal the essence.
Ignore the blandishments and lures.
Keep your mind calm and focused.
Find your truth.

'One hour of contemplation surpasses sixty years of worship.'
Muhammad (570AD-632AD)

Observe

.

Most of us see, few observe.
Foster the art of observation.
Use your eyes like a great cameraman:
with wide, receptive eyes and an open mind.
Mix sweeping wide shots, with tight close-ups.
Look high, look low.
Seek marginal differences, mismatches.
But don't overlook the obvious.

'The power of accurate observation is commonly
called cynicism by those who have not got it.'
George Bernard Shaw (1856-1950)

Learn from the past

How can you know where you're heading,
if you don't know where you've come from?
Isolate the lessons from the journey.
So many of the answers to future questions,
are held in your past experiences.
Value them, use them.

'Bring the past only if you're going to build from it.'
Domenico Cieri Estrada (1954-)

Forget your age

Live as though you have no idea of your age.
The primes of our lives come at different stages.
You're only old if you surrender your dreams.
After all, who says you have to play by set rules.
Live by the day ...
the years will take care of themselves.

'Everyone is the age of their heart.'

Guatemalan proverb

Break out

At times we all find ourselves in a rut.
That's when we may have to look at things differently.
If you can change your circumstances, do so.
If you can't, then try a different viewpoint.
Before you can break out,
you need to realise where you're confined.

'Habit reflects the unreflecting herd.'
William Wordsworth (1770-1850)

Foster talent

It's such a precious commodity.
It can bring so much joy ...
yet so much sadness when wasted or ignored.
When you see talent
treat it with respect, help it grow.
Enjoy the inspiration as it blossoms.

'Like the moon, come out from behind the clouds.'
Gautama Buddha (563BC-483BC)

Reject mediocrity

Think of the things you've achieved when you had to.
How far you've pushed yourself under duress.
Recall the satisfaction at exceeding your expectations.
And the way it inspired you to greater effort.
Never settle for just OK when you can push further.
Aim high.

'Mediocrity is a hand-rail.'

Baron de Montesquieu (1689-1755)

Soften your heart

Take every chance to lighten the day.
Look through gentle eyes.
Feel for others, sense their emotions.
It will make your journey so much richer.
And take your mind off your troubles.
You'll feel the warmth flow back to you.

'Be kind whenever possible. It is always possible.'
Tenzin Gyatso, 14th Dalai Lama (1935-)

Use sleep

It's nature's balm ...
a matchless elixir for body and mind.
Make sure you don't scrimp on it.
Welcome its soothing embrace.
Surrender to its restorative powers.
Awake rejuvenated.

'Finish each day before you begin the next and interpose
a solid wall of sleep between the two.'

Ralph Waldo Emerson (1803-1882)

Make notes

So many good ideas are lost ...
in the no-man's-land between the
mind and the record.
Whether it's a journal, a notebook or a screen,
record your important thoughts.
Re-reading them often reignites them ...
or transforms them into something extraordinary.

'The way to get good ideas is to get lots of
ideas, and throw the bad ones away.'

Linus Pauling (1901-1994)

Eat breakfast

It really is the most important meal of your day.
Not just nutritionally, but also spiritually.
It centres you before you start your day's adventures.
It allows you to pause and reflect
on your night's thoughts.
It connects you with your family.
It empowers you to meet the challenges ahead.

'Never work before breakfast; if you have to work
before breakfast, eat your breakfast first.'

Josh Billings (1818-1885)

Laugh

Is there any better medicine ... for body or soul?
A belly laugh brings an infusion
of therapeutic warmth,
that reaches every nook in the body
It massages tired muscles ... and unknots stresses.
It sends you on a mini-holiday.
And it spreads wellness in the air.

'Laughter is a tranquilizer with no side effects.'
Arnold Glasow (1905-1998)

Hug a lot

A hug stands alone.
It doesn't even need words,
although the right ones add to it immensely.
Hugging heals.
It transfers love and hope.
A single hug can change a life.

'The way to love anything is to realise that it may be lost.'
G. K. Chesterton (1874-1936)

Be a mentor

We can all help others as mentors.
You don't have to be an expert.
Act as a sounding board.
Draw on your common sense and life experience.
Give of them freely.
Your accumulated wisdom can enhance lives.
It can even save lives.

'When you learn, teach; when you get, give.'

Maya Angelou (1928-)

Timeshift to live

Break free from the thralldom of programming.
Take control of scheduling your entertainment.
Record, or download your favourites ...
then play them in your own time.
Use the ensuing freedom to actively live your life ...
and to expand your knowledge.

'Time! The corrector when our judgements err.'
Lord Byron (1788-1824)

Volunteer

Volunteers are rewarded handsomely.
Not with money, but with satisfaction and gratitude:
the satisfaction of knowing they have
improved their world;
the gratitude from those whose lives they have helped.
Whatever you give as a volunteer ...
is returned with incalculable interest.

'Wherever a man turns he can find someone who needs him.'
Albert Schweitzer (1875-1965)

Trust your kids

There is no such thing as a normal childhood.
We are each dealt different hands.
In many ways our parents determine
how we play them.
Do your best to give your kids access to knowledge.
Add what wisdom you can.
Trust them to make their own decisions.

'What's done to children, they will do to society'
Karl Menninger (1893-1990)

Listen to your family

It's where we start ... and usually where we end.
Our family is a microcosm of our lives.
Hidden in that maelstrom of madness ...
are many gems of accumulated wisdom.
Don't discount the importance of family,
or their support.
In times of trouble, seek their counsel.

'Rejoice with your family in the beautiful land of life.'
Albert Einstein (1879-1955)

Conquer stress

Stress is toxic.
It's exacerbated by inertia.
Adopt the theory:
change what you can,
accept what you can't,
learn to differentiate between the two.
Often just taking action will alleviate stress.
It's often easier said than done ...
but just as often it's doable.

'People become attached to their burdens sometimes
more than the burdens are attached to them.'
George Bernard Shaw (1856-1950)

Spend time with your partner

We all need somebody to share with:
a partner with our interests in their heart.
The stories shared are more vibrant.
The views shared are more beautiful.
The sorrows shared are lighter.
Time spent with your loved one …
earns double life frequent-flyer points.

'I find it shelter to speak to you.'

Emily Dickinson (1830-1886)

Look past the detail

Every so often you must lift your head.
Look above the crowd, find the horizon.
Get your bearings, set your compass.
Details are important but they can swamp you.
Aim to keep the big picture in mind.
Gauge your success and your progress ...
on a large-scale map.

'You can never cross the ocean unless you have
the courage to lose sight of the shore.'
Christopher Columbus (1451-1506)

Embrace silence

In silence we find our inner thoughts,
without the distortions of daily life.
Silence, in nature's beauty, inspires true awe.
Find the quiet to hear yourself.
Treat it like a tonic.
Allow it to refresh and replenish your spirit.

'Silence is the mother of truth.'

Benjamin Disraeli (1804-1881)

Don't save it for later

If you're constantly waiting for the perfect time,
you'll usually miss the right time.
Err on the spontaneous side:
trust your intuition, go with the flow.
Use your wisdom, earned from the past,
But the future is already starting.

'And in today already walks tomorrow.'
Samuel Taylor Coleridge (1772-1834)

Walk on a beach

Feel the mesmeric monotony of eternal waves,
all unharnessed rhythmic energy.
Walk barefoot in the wet sand at water's edge,
where the sand sucks in its life force.
Breathe deeply the swirling salt-filled air.
Watch the spindrift dancing on the breakers.
Let the earth's history surround you.

'Adopt the pace of nature, her secret is patience.'
Ralph Waldo Emerson (1803-1882)

Deliver on your promises

Be the exception: make your word your bond.
We all know how rare you'll be.
Most of us commit with the right intentions.
How many actually deliver?
Be one of the select few who honours their word.
Delay makes it harder.
Do it as soon as you can.

'Promise little and do much.'

Hebrew Proverb

Show gratitude

When thanks are due, go out of your way to give them.
But, more than that, mean it.
It's not simply good manners.
It honours your benefactor.
It makes sense of the act.
It frees your spirit.
It encourages repetition of the kindness.

'Gratitude is the fairest blossom which springs from the soul.'
Henry Ward Beecher (1813-1887)

Explore art

Art allows us to view another's soul.
To see things through another's eyes.
True artists expose some of their innermost feelings.
They give us a glimpse of the creative spark.
Their virtuosity opens doors in our imagination.
They stir our creative juices.

'I dream my painting and I paint my dream.'
Vincent van Gogh (1853-1890)

Count your blessings

It's not so complicated:
you can view your life positively or negatively.
You can appreciate what you have ...
or spend your energy coveting more.
It's tempting to decry your situation.
But more sensible to accept reality as a base ...
be thankful for it ...
and work to better it.

'May you live all the days of your life.'

Jonathan Swift (1667-1745)

Use active voice

Its where the subject of your sentence
performs the action.
It may sound trivial or technical ...
but it will transform your writing.
It will bring it alive.
It will give it power, pace and flow.
In your writing, whatever the subject,
make active voice your default.

'Writing is a struggle against silence.'

Carlos Fuentes (1928-2012)

Make the most of you

Tell your story

Be the writer/director of your own life story.
Be the poet and the poem.
Be proud of where you've come from,
your achievements and your aspirations.
Tell your story in the way you live.

'There is just one life for each of us: our own.'

Euripides (480BC-406BC)

Play with your ideas

When you come up with a concept, evaluate it.
Challenge it, embellish it, expand it.
If you can use it immediately, do so.
If you can combine it with others, do so.
But if not, don't reject and discard it.
Record it and let it lie fallow.
Many ideas have second and third lives.

'No problem can withstand the assault of sustained thinking.'
Voltaire (Francois-Marie Arouet) (1694-1778)

Look beyond your world

We're each constrained by our experiences,
but not by our imagination or our intellect.
In confronting problems,
we usually draw on what is familiar,
limiting the potential solutions.
Far better to extend our gaze beyond
our normal domain,
vastly increasing our chances of finding an answer.

'We all live under the same sky, but we
don't all have the same horizon.'

Konrad Adenauer (1876-1967)

Look them in the eye

A forthright response can transform a situation.
If you believe in your position,
let your body language reflect it.
Fix your opponents with unflinching eyes.
Look into their minds.
Challenge them to match your conviction.

'One of the most wonderful things in nature is a glance of the eye;
it transcends speech; it is the bodily symbol of identity.'
Ralph Waldo Emerson (1803-1882)

Use all your gears

Good cyclists use all of a bike's capacity.
Thus they draw the best from themselves.
We can learn when to coast ...
and when to change gears for the tough climbs.
If you don't change gears to suit the terrain,
you'll never discover how far or fast you can go.

'Most of us have gears we never use.'

Charles Schulz (1922-2000)

Find the wonder

It's all around us if we look for it …
in the squeals of delight of playing children,
in the warmth of a lover's embrace,
in the first rays of a new dawn.
Find it, draw hope and inspiration from it.
Let it power your day.

'In every real man a child is hidden that wants to play.'
Friedrich Nietzsche (1844-1900)

Follow your instincts

If you think back on them ...
most of our best decisions were made instinctively.
We drew on our spiritual and experiential wisdom.
We trusted our feelings, as well as our minds.
Life leads us to file away knowledge,
we can use almost subconsciously when needed.
Trust yourself to use it properly.

'I would rather trust a woman's instinct than a man's reason.'
Stanley Baldwin (1867-1947)

Make your own rules

Not all rules are created equal.
Nor are all even intended to be equal.
While justice is an admirable aspiration …
it's administered by fallible humans
We almost always know what is fair.
We should reserve the right to decide for ourselves.

'The more corrupt the republic, the more numerous the laws.'
Tacitus (56AD-117AD)

Use your Imagination

We all have it but some let it fall into disuse.
Use every chance to set it free.
It will help in all aspects of your life:
it will open opportunities beyond cold reasoning.
It can come in a rush, or slowly
awaken without fanfare.
But we must allow it to soar ...
and be receptive to its fantasies.

'I saw the angel in the marble and carved until I set him free.'
Michelangelo (1475-1564)

Take it gradually

Experience teaches us how to pace ourselves:
to slow down, to savour the situation,
or to regather our forces.
It's one of life's most valuable lessons.
It prevents many disasters.
It unveils many discoveries.

'Nature does not hurry, yet everything is accomplished.'
Lao Tzu (around 400BC)

Don't learn by rote

Rather than endlessly memorising ...
absorb knowledge and learn where to find it.
This is especially true in the digital age,
where so much is just a click away.
Use the amazing capacity of the net
to take a broad view.
But make sure you're learning from good sources.

'Never memorize something that you can look up.'
Albert Einstein (1879-1955)

Be the you that you admire

Within each of us lies our best self:
the sum of our finest characteristics.
In there too is our worst self.
The two vie for top billing.
Our best self provides the template, the ideal model.
It's our best guide to improvement …
For nobody really knows us better than ourselves.

'And remember, no matter where you go, there you are.'
Confucius (551BC-479BC)

Move forward each day

Don't mark time while waiting for a big breakthrough.
Try to chalk up some progress each day.
Build momentum and confidence
by taking small steps.
Resolve the small things.
This will shine a light on the main obstacles.
It will expose new possibilities.

'Better to take many small steps in the right direction than
to make a great leap forward only to stumble backward.'
Chinese proverb